VOLCANOES & EARTHQUAKES, WHAT & WHY?: 2ND GRADE SCIENCE SERIES

Earthquakes and volcanic eruptions happen at the boundaries between plates.

VOLCANOES

Volcanoes are openings
in the Earth's surface. When
they are active they can let ash,
gas and hot magma escape
in sometimes violent and
spectacular eruptions.

Volcanoes
are formed when
magma from within the
Earth's upper mantle works its
way to the surface. It erupts to
form lava flows and ash deposits.
As the volcano continues to
erupt, it will get bigger
and bigger.

Lava and Magma are
both molten rock. Magma
is liquid rock inside a volcano.
Lava is liquid rock that flows
out of a volcano.

EARTHQUAKES

Earthquakes are the rumblings, shaking or rolling of the earth's surface. They are the Earth's natural means of releasing stress. More than a million earthquakes shake the world each year.

There are about 20
plates along the surface
of the earth. The plates
constantly move. Earthquakes
happen when a plate scrapes,
bumps, or drags along
another plate.

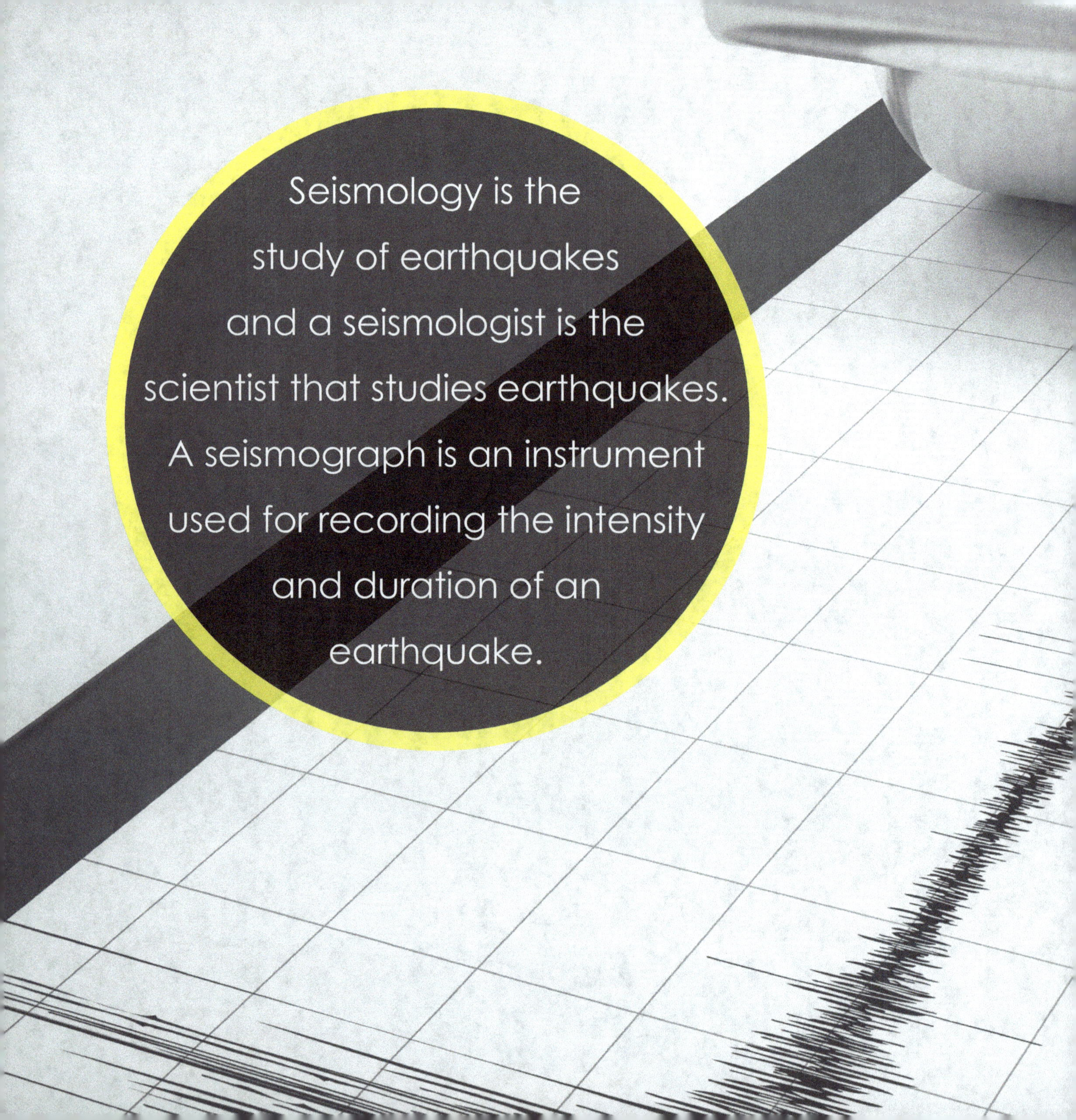

Seismology is the
study of earthquakes
and a seismologist is the
scientist that studies earthquakes.
A seismograph is an instrument
used for recording the intensity
and duration of an
earthquake.

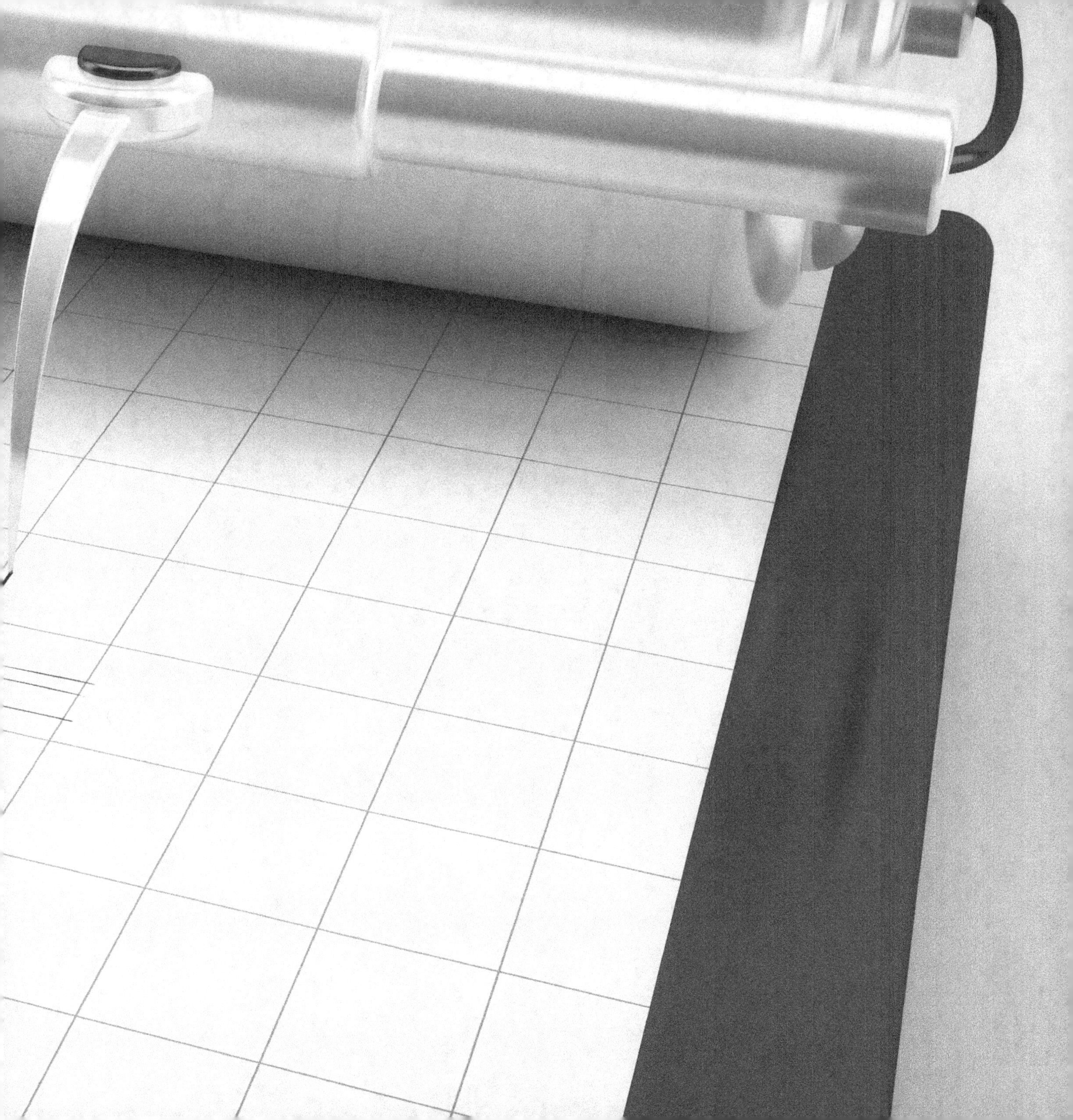